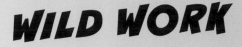

WILD WORK

Who Lands Planes on a Ship?

WORKING ON AN AIRCRAFT CARRIER

Linda Tagliaferro

Raintree

Chicago, Illinois

www.heinemannraintree.com
Visit our website to find out more information about Heinemann-Raintree books.

To order:
☎ Phone 888-454-2279
💻 Visit www.heinemannraintree.com to browse our catalog and order online.

© 2011 Raintree
an imprint of Capstone Global Library, LLC
Chicago, Illinois

Edited by David Andrews, Nancy Dickmann, and Rebecca Rissman
Designed by Victoria Allen
Picture research by Liz Alexander
Leveled by Marla Conn, with Read-Ability.
Originated by Dot Gradations Ltd
Printed and bound in China by Leo Paper Products

15 14 13 12 11 10
10 9 8 7 6 5 4 3 2 1

Library of Congress Cataloging-in-Publication Data

Tagliaferro, Linda.
  Who lands planes on a ship? : working on an aircraft carrier / Linda Tagliaferro.
     p. cm.—(Wild work)
  Includes bibliographical references and index.
  ISBN 978-1-4109-3853-4 (hc)—ISBN 978-1-4109-3862-6 (pb) 1. Aircraft carriers—Juvenile literature. 2. Aircraft carriers—Flight decks—Juvenile literature. I. Title.
  V874.3.T34 2011
  359.9' 435—dc22   2009050293

Acknowledgements

The author and publisher are grateful to the following for permission to reproduce copyright material:

Alamy pp. 5 (© Purestock), 8 (© Richard Cooke), 21 (© H. Mark Weidman Photography); Corbis pp. 11 (© Chad Hunt), 12 (© Ron Sachs/CNP/Sygma), 17, 19 (© Corbis Sygma), 28 (© U.S. Navy - digital version copy/Science Faction); Defense Imagery pp. 7 (MC3 Kilho Park), 13 (MCSA Jessica Ellington), 14 (MC3 Josue L. Escobosa), 15 (MC3 Christopher Baker), 22 (MCSN Robert Winn), 25 (MCSN Donald R. White Jr.); Getty Images pp. 4 (Check Six), 16 (Dibyangshu Sarkar/AFP), 18 (U.S. Navy), 23 (Koichi Kamoshida), 24 (Time & Life Pictures), 26 (Joe Raedle); Photolibrary pp. 9 (Northrop Grumman/Index Stock Imagery), 10 (PureStock), 27 (StockTrek Corporation/ Superstock); Shutterstock pp. 6 (© Horst Kanzek), 20 (© Philip Lange), 29 (© dcwcreations); background images (© Kletr).

Cover photograph reproduced with permission of Getty Images (Kittie VandenBosch-U.S. Navy).

Every effort has been made to contact copyright holders of any material reproduced in this book. Any omissions will be rectified in subsequent printings if notice is given to the publisher.

Disclaimer

Some words are shown in bold, **like this**. You can find out what they mean by looking in the glossary.

Contents

Sudden Landing!

A speeding plane comes in for a landing on a ship. Will it stop in time? Or will it splash into the ocean? Suddenly, a hook on the plane catches wires on the ship. The plane stops in time!

hook

DID YOU KNOW?

An airplane is moving at 150 miles (240 km) per hour when it starts to land. But it stops in just two seconds!

Floating Cities

Aircaft carriers are big **warships** that planes can land on. Planes fly to and from the aircraft carrier to protect a country and fight enemies. Thousands of people live and work on these ships. They are like small cities.

An aircraft carrier has enough room for a basketball court!

Who Lands a Plane on a Ship?

Navy **pilots** have exciting jobs. But landing on aircraft carriers can be scary. Pilots train, or practice, landing on aircraft carriers. They also practice taking off!

DID YOU KNOW?

Pilots wait to hear from the aircraft carrier that it is safe to land.

Into Enemy Territory!

Pilots on aircraft carriers help their country fight wars. They fly planes over enemy land. They find out what the enemy is doing. They can drop **bombs** from the air to destroy enemies. Pilots also help to protect people.

Pilots in planes help protect soldiers on the ground.

The Flight Deck

The top level of an aircraft carrier is called the **flight deck**. Workers on the flight deck use a machine called a **catapult**. It helps blast airplanes into the sky.

DID YOU KNOW?

An aircraft carrier can hold 80 planes!

DID YOU KNOW?

It only takes two seconds for a catapult to send a plane zooming off.

catapult

Some say the flight deck is one of the most dangerous places in the world. Planes with weapons are always zooming by. The **catapult** officer guides the pilots using body signals.

Aircraft Carrier Body Signals

- Raised fists mean "brakes on."

- Leaning forward and pointing means "launch."

Preparing Planes

The **hangar deck** is below the **flight deck**. It is like a big garage for airplanes. Many people work on the hangar deck. Mechanics fix planes. Workers pump fuel into airplanes. Some workers bring planes up to the flight deck on elevators.

elevator

DID YOU KNOW?

U.S. Navy workers who pump fuel into planes wear purple shirts. They are called "grapes."

Powerful Weapons

Aircraft carriers are **warships**. They need **weapons** to protect the ship. The people who work with weapons have very dangerous jobs. Workers carefully load weapons onto planes.

Some weapons can explode if they aren't handled carefully!

The Air Boss

A tall building called an island is on one end of the aircraft carrier. A person called the **air boss** directs takeoffs and landings here. As many as two planes per minute can take off. The air boss must always pay attention.

island

Who's in Control?

About 5,000 men and women live on an aircraft carrier. They sail for months before returning to land. Someone must make sure everyone does their job.

The **captain** is the leader of the ship. Everyone follows the captain's orders.

Caring for Sick People

Doctors live and work on an aircraft carrier. They take care of everyone's health. There is even a hospital on the ship. If someone is very sick or hurt in battle, doctors can perform operations.

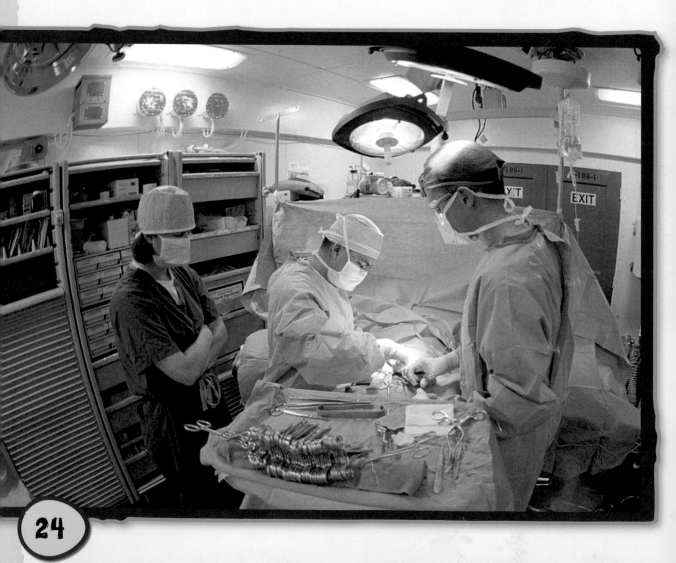

Airplane pilots must have perfect vision. This doctor is testing his patient's eyesight.

To the Rescue!

Everyone on a ship is careful. But accidents can still happen. Aircraft carriers must be ready for **emergencies**. They even have firefighters on the ship! If a fire starts, these firefighters can quickly put it out.

Helicopters rescue
people who fall into
the ocean.

Could You Work on an Aircraft Carrier?

Would you like living on a floating city? Do you think and act quickly in **emergencies**? To become a **pilot**, you have to work and study hard for many years. It's worth it if you want the thrill of flying speeding planes onto an aircraft carrier.

DANGER
EJECTION SEAT
&
CANOPY

DANGER

A CARTRIDGE-
SYSTEM
GES. SEE
FOR

E
EXTERNAL POW
RECEPTACLE

29

Glossary

air boss the person on an aircraft carrier who directs airplane takeoffs and landings

bomb a weapon that explodes

captain the person in charge on an aircraft carrier

catapult a machine that helps to get an airplane into the sky from an aircraft carrier

emergencies situations that are sudden and serious

flight deck the top level of an aircraft carrier where planes take off and land

hangar deck a deck, or level, of an aircraft carrier where airplanes are stored

pilot a person who flies an airplane

warship large ship made especially for fighting

weapon something used to harm others or protect yourself

Find Out More

Books to Read

Peterson, Tiffany. *Watercraft*. Chicago: Heinemann-Raintree, 2008.

Roza, Greg. *The Incredible Story of Aircraft Carriers*. New York: PowerKids Press, 2004.

Stone, Lynn M. *Aircraft Carriers*. Vero Beach, FL: Rourke, 2007.

Web Sites to Visit

Aircraft Carrier *USS Hornet* Museum
http://www.uss-hornet.org
Learn about an aircraft carrier that is now a museum in California.

Northrop Grumman's USS *George H.W. Bush* page
http://www.nn.northropgrumman.com/bush/kids.html
Just for kids, this website has fun facts about aircraft carriers and even a downloadable coloring book.

Index